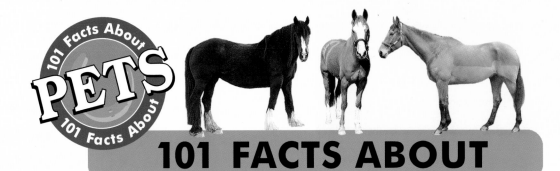

101 Facts About PETS
101 Facts About

101 FACTS ABOUT

HORSES & PONIES

Published by Ringpress Books Limited,
PO Box 8, Lydney, Gloucestershire,
GL15 4YN, United Kingdom.

Design: Sara Howell

First Published 2001
© 2001 RINGPRESS BOOKS LIMITED

ISBN 1 86054 236 0

Printed in Hong Kong through Printworks Int. Ltd

0 9 8 7 6 5 4 3 2 1

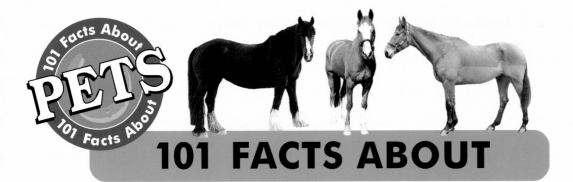

101 Facts About PETS
101 Facts About

101 FACTS ABOUT

HORSES
& PONIES

Julia Barnes

Ringpress Books

1 Horses are great survivors – they have a history going back an amazing 50 million years. When conditions changed, the horse changed with them.

2 The first horses had padded, three-toed feet and short legs. But when the climate cooled (5-23 million years ago), and the landscape changed to open grasslands, the horse was in danger.

30119 022 710 968

**This book is to be returned on or before
the last date stamped below.**

2 4 APR 2004	2 0 APR 2005	
1 4 AUG 2004	1 3 AUG 2005	
2 4 SEP 2004	2 4 MAY 2006	
1 5 OCT 2004		
0 4 DEC 2004	0 3 APR 2014	
2 6 FEB 2005	2 9 JAN 2015	
	2 3 JUL 2015	

LEARNING FOR LIFE
LONDON BOROUGH OF SUTTON LIBRARIES

RENEWALS   Please quote: date of return, your ticket number
and computer label number for each item.

3 There was nowhere to hide from his enemies, so the horse needed to be fast enough to escape. He developed long legs and single hooves for galloping.

4 There were a number of horse-type animals living around the world, but it was a family called **Equus** that proved to be the best survivor.

5 The fastest and the fittest, Equus grew in numbers until he became the only type of horse left.

6 The Equus family is divided into two main groups: **hot-bloods** and **cold-bloods**.

7 In the hot, dry regions, a lightly-built, fast horse developed, which became known as a hot-blood.

slow-moving, they lived in the harshest of conditions.

10 The smallest animals in the cold-blood group developed into pony breeds (pictured far right).

8 The **Arab** breed comes from this group. An Arab (pictured above) has a fine coat, a high-set tail, and a long head, with large nostrils to breathe out the dusty air.

9 The cold-bloods (pictured right) lived further north. Big, heavy and

11 The horses and ponies we know today have changed very little since the time they lived in herds on huge, grass plains.

12 As hunted animals, horses had to be alert for the tiniest hint of danger, so, over millions of years, they have developed special ways of detecting trouble.

13 A horse has enormous eyes, and he has near all-round vision.

14 There are only two blind spots, one is immediately behind the horse, the other is just in front of, and beneath, the nose.

17 Each ear can work on its own (pictured below), so your pony can listen to what is going on around him with one ear, while the other checks out a more distant sound.

15 Horses can also see well at night, which was important if an enemy tried to creep up on the herd.

16 The ears are set high on the head, and can move in all directions to pick up sounds.

8

18 The horse uses his sense of smell to detect if an enemy is approaching, and to check that there are no poisonous plants in the grass.

19 A horse cannot be caught napping by his enemies so he will sleep for just 2 to 5 hours a day, and he will only do this in short spells.

20 For a light sleep, the horse will remain standing, but he will lie down for a deeper sleep (right).

21 In the wild, a male horse (a **stallion**), looks after and protects his herd of females (**mares**).

22 The top-ranking boss mare controls the other mares and the youngsters, and decides when the herd should move on.

25 Male foals **(colts)** are driven away by the stallion when they are about 18 months. They form all-male herds.

23 Newborn **foals** must keep up with the herd. For this reason, they can stand within an hour of being born.

26 A strong, young stallion may challenge an older stallion to take over his herd, or he may start his own herd.

24 Female foals **(fillies)** stay with the herd for a couple of years, and then they usually drift off to start their own families.

27 To begin with, humans hunted horses for their meat. But it did not take them long to realise how useful horses could be in other ways.

28 There are drawings from ancient civilizations dating back to 2000 BC which show horses being ridden and harnessed to chariots.

29 Today, there are around 200 horse and pony breeds in the world.

30 These breeds have been developed to carry out different tasks.

31 Horses and ponies come in all shapes and sizes. A horse's height is measured in **hands**. One hand measures 4 ins (10.2 cms).

33 The smallest horse on record was called Little Pumpkin, who measured 14 ins (3.2 hands).

34 The Shire (pictured below) is the biggest horse breed. He is used for ploughing fields and for pulling heavy carts.

32 The world's smallest horse is the Falabella (pictured above). They are bred as pets, and measure just 8.2 hands (34 ins) at the shoulder.

37 Most ponies are very strong. They have short legs, and they move with short, quick strides.

38 They are generally 'good doers' – they do well on very little food, and can withstand the cold.

35 The world's biggest Shire was called Mammouth. He measured 21.2 hands (85 ins).

39 Ponies are famous for being quick-thinking – as you will probably find when you are learning to ride!

36 A pony (pictured above) is 14.2 hands or under, but ponies are not just 'little horses' they have a number of special features.

40 The Shetland pony comes from the Shetland and Orkney Islands in Scotland.

41 Small but strong, the Shetland (pictured below) was the farmer's all-round helpmate. He carried fuel for fires, seaweed to fertilise the field, and was also used to pull a plough.

42 The Dales pony (pictured above), from the north-east of England, had to go underground and work in the mines, pulling heavy carts of coal.

43 In Norway, the Vikings rode Norwegian Fjord ponies into battle. In times of peace, they were used for farm work.

44 Today, there are a few ponies that are still used on the farm, but most are bred for children to ride and enjoy.

45 The heavy, working horse breeds include the Shire, the Percheron, the Ardennes, the Clydesdale (pictured right), and the Suffolk Punch. They are known as the gentle giants of the horse world.

46 They are slow-moving, easygoing types, who have used their great strength and pulling power to work for man.

47 As modern machinery took over the horse's role, these breeds were in danger of dying out. Thankfully, breeders have worked hard to save them.

48 The horse has always been used as a means of transport, either being ridden or pulling a carriage.

49 In more recent times, the horse has developed a new role as a sports competitor.

50 Horse sports range from the thrills of racing and **cross-country** jumping events, to the skills of **dressage**, which test the horse's ability to perform flatwork exercises.

51 The Arab is the oldest and purest of all the horse breeds, with a history dating back to 3000 BC.

52 The beautiful Arab, with his narrow head, flowing mane, and perfectly balanced body is used for racing.

55 Although it is the best-known breed, the Thoroughbred is fairly new to the horse world. It was developed in England, in the 1700s.

53 It is also best at **endurance** riding (pictured above), where horse and rider compete over long distances, some-times over a number of days.

56 Thoroughbred bloodlines have been mixed with many other breeds to produce fast, good-looking horses.

54 The Thoroughbred was developed as the perfect racing machine, and the breed is used to run on the flat and over fences at racecourses all over the world.

58 The USA has produced a number of its own horse breeds. The Quarter Horse (pictured below) is its oldest breed, and is famous for its amazing sprinting ability.

59 The Quarter Horse can go from a standing start to 40 miles an hour in a single stride.

57 The Andalusian (Spanish horse), and the world famous Lipizzaner (pictured above) – are famous for their classical riding skills which they perform in front of huge crowds.

He can cover a distance of a quarter of a mile in just 21 seconds.

60 The fastest Quarter Horse racehorses have clocked speeds of 55 miles an hour!

61 The Morgan (pictured right) is America's most beautiful horse with his proud, classical looks, and his brave spirit.

62 The Morgan was the official horse of the US Army and is still used by many police squads today.

63 Horses come in many different colours with a range of markings.

64 In the US, there are four colours which are classed as separate breeds. They are Palamino, Appaloosa, Albino, and Pinto.

65 The Palamino (pictured below) has a glorious gold coat with a pale mane and tail. This breed is used for the American style of Western riding.

66 Spotted horses (Appaloosas) (pictured right) are spectacular to look at. They were the favourite horse of North American Nez Perce Indians.

67 There are eight Appaloosa coat patterns. Including: Snowflake (dark with white spots) and Leopard (white with dark spots).

68 Even though Appaloosas come in different patterns, each horse has its own special markings, which means no two horses look the same.

69 Albino horses have no pigment (colour-ing). Their coats are white, and they have very sensitive pink skin and blue eyes.

71 Other horse colours include black, **bay** (brown with a black mane and tail), chestnut, and grey (ranging from deep iron-grey to pure white).

72 A **roan** horse has a spread of white hairs within the coat. A 'strawberry' roan has a chestnut coat.

70 The **Pinto** or **Paint Horse** (pictured right) with its dramatic broken colouring, was loved by the American Indians, and later by the cowboys of the Wild West.

21

75 A white mark between the nostrils is called a **snip**. A white mark on the forehead is known as a star (pictured right).

76 A white marking on the leg which reaches just above the fetlock (ankle) is known as

73 A **dun** horse (pictured above) has a light-coloured coat with a black mane and tail.

74 Horses may have white markings. A narrow white stripe down the middle of the face is called a **stripe**. A broad white stripe is called a blaze (pictured right).

a **sock**. A stocking (pictured below left) reaches to the knee or hock.

77 You will get on better with the pony you ride if you can understand 'horse language'.

78 An alert horse (pictured right) has his ears pricked forwards, and will look bright and attentive.

79 A contented horse will have a dreamy look. His ears will be slightly droopy, and his top lip may come over his bottom lip.

80 A frightened horse will have his eyes wide open; he may even show the whites of his eyes. His nostrils will be flared, and his ears may be pinned back.

83 In the wild, horses groom themselves with their teeth, and they will also groom other members of the herd (pictured right).

84 In a domestic situation, we need to groom the coat every day, using special brushes.

85 The mane and tail need particular attention. At shows, they are often plaited.

81 An angry horse (pictured above) will flatten his ears and may show his teeth.

82 Horses love to roll (pictured right). It eases itchy places, and it also gets the 'herd scent' on to their coats.

88 It is important that you know the right way to behave around horses so you don't frighten them.

86 The horse's hooves must also be looked after. The mud should be picked out from the underside of the hooves every day.

89 Never run around or shout when you are near horses. They are easily startled, and will 'spook' (pictured below) if they get a sudden shock.

87 Most ridden horses wear shoes on their feet. The farrier will come every six weeks or so to trim the hooves and fit new shoes.

90 Do not walk directly behind a horse. The horse cannot see you, and may kick if he feels threatened.

91 Try to be calm and confident when you are around horses. This makes them feel safe, and they will learn to trust you.

92 If you want to give a treat, offer it on the palm of your hand, so the horse can get hold of it without biting.

93 Horses and ponies that are used for riding must get used to wearing the equipment or **tack** which is used for riding.

94 The basic tack is a **saddle** for the rider to sit on, and a **bridle** (pictured right) which fits on the horse's head.

96 The bit sits on the gums in a gap between the incisor 'biting' teeth at the front and molar or 'grinding' teeth at the back.

95 The horse is trained to wear a **bit**, which fits in his mouth and is attached to the reins.

97 If you want to learn to ride, find a good riding school where the horses are well looked after, and where all the instructors are fully qualified.

98 There are lots of different pony activities you can try. When you have mastered riding on the flat, you may want to try jumping (pictured left).

99 At some shows there are fancy dress classes (pictured right) where you and your pony can go in for a spectacular double act.

100 Mounted games, which include bending races, egg-and-spoon races, and flag

101 But you don't have to enter a competition to have fun. The best times of all can be spent riding on trails, or simply helping to look after your pony.

races, are great fun for both pony and rider. You can also try showing your pony, where a judge gives marks for the way your pony looks, and for how you ride him.

GLOSSARY

Albino: no colour pigment.

Appaloosa: spotted horse.

Bay: brown horse with black mane and tail.

Bit: fits in a horse's mouth and is attached to the reins.

Bridle: fits over the horse's head.

Cold-bloods: horses from cold regions.

Colt: a young, male horse or pony.

Cross-country: jumping over solid fences in open country.

Dressage: flatwork competition.

Dun: light coat, black points.

Endurance: where a horse and rider compete over long distances.

Equus: the name for the horse family.

Filly: a young, female horse or pony.

Foal: a baby horse or pony.

Hands: unit for measuring height.

Hot-bloods: horses from hot, dry regions.

Mare: a female horse or pony.

Palamino: a gold coat and a pale mane and tail.

Pinto/Paint: broken colouring.

Roan: a spread of white hairs within the main body coat.

Saddle: for the rider to sit on.

Snip: white mark between the nostrils.

Sock: white mark which reaches just above the ankle.

Stallion: a male horse or pony.

Stripe: a white stripe down the middle of the face.

MORE BOOKS TO READ

Horse and Pony Guides to:
Better Riding; Horse And Pony
Care; Horse And Pony Breeds;
Jumping; Tack And How To Use It;
Understanding Ponies.
Jackie Budd
(Ringpress Books)

Your Pony, Your Horse
Cherry Hill
(Storey Books)

Let's Ride
Linda Tellington-Jones
(Trafalgar Square)

WEBSITES

Equiworld index
www.equiworld.net/horselinks/

Horse club
www.horseclub.co.uk/

Bernie's yard
http://takeoff.to/berniesyard

Pony club
www.pony-club.org.uk/

To find additional websites, use a reliable search engine to find one or more of the following key words: **horses**, **ponies**, **pony care**, **horse care**, **pony riding**.

INDEX